Your Top Air Fryer Recipe Book

Amazing Family Meals And Snacks For Everyone To Enjoy

Sammy Pommel

ISBN - 9798841352686

Table of Contents

EXCLUSIVE BONUS

40 Weight Loss Recipes

&

14 Days Meal Plan

Scan the QR-Code and receive
the FREE download:

Introduction

You've probably heard of the new appliance everyone is talking about and have decided to see what the fuss is for yourself. Well, you've come to the right place! With this book, you'll be excited to learn just how easy it is to get started with an Air Fryer. Soon, you'll be hooked and using your Air Fryer to prepare nearly every meal. But what is it that makes air frying so special?

An Air Fryer is a countertop appliance that can replace your oven, microwave, deep fryer and dehydrator to evenly cook delicious meals in minutes. Cooking with an Air Fryer is just as easy as using a microwave. No need to preheat, once you have your ingredients prepared, you simply load them into the Air Fryer, set the temperature and/or time, and then come back to a deliciously prepared meal.

If you are looking to serve your family healthy meals but don't have a lot of time to stand over a pan of hot oil an Air Fryer is just what you need. Throughout this book, you'll learn everything you need to know about how and why to use an Air Fryer as well as some tips and tricks to help you get the most out of your Air Fryer.

What Is Air Frying?

Air frying is achieved by circulating hot air inside the Air Fryer chamber typically with a basket filled with ingredients.

The Air Fryer's cooking chamber induces heat from a heating element next to the food. Then, a heavy-duty fan ensures hot air reaches every surface of the food you are cooking to create a crispy, golden brown surface. The opening at the top of the Air Fryer, or vent, allows hot air to be taken in and the exhaust at the back controls temperature by releasing excess hot air. It is also used to counter any increases in internal pressure.

Conventional frying methods involve submerging foods in hot oil, which reaches considerably higher temperatures than boiling water. The Air Fryer works by coating the desired food in a thin layer of oil while circulating air heated up to apply heat and initiate the reaction. As a result, the appliance can brown foods like potato chips, chicken, fish, steak, cheeseburgers, French fries or pastries using 70% to 80% less oil than a traditional deep fryer.

Many Air Fryers have temperature and timer adjustments that allow more precise cooking. Food is cooked in a cooking basket that sits atop a drip tray. The basket and the food inside must be shaken frequently to ensure even oil treatment and cooking. More expensive fryers achieve this by mixing a food agitator that continuously shakes the food during the cooking process. However, most Air Fryers require the cook to perform the task manually. Convection ovens and Air Fryers are similar in the way they cook food, but Air Fryers are mostly smaller in size and volume than convection ovens and emit less heat.

The taste and consistency of foods cooked with traditional fried methods in comparison to air fried methods are not the same, because the larger quantity of oil involved in traditional frying soaks into the foods (or the coating batter, if it is used) and adds its unique flavour. With Air Fryers, food is coated in a wet batter and stays firmly on the food surface, meaning the Air Fryer's fan can blow the batter off the food and evenly cook all surfaces of the food. As long as you don't overfill the Air Fryer or overcook your food, it will be tender and juicy inside. It is also important not to put oil inside the Air Fryer or have flammable objects near the Air Fryer. The taste of air fried food is not heavy and greasy like deep fried food but lighter and crispier.

Air fryers are fast, and once you understand how they work, they can be used to cook all sorts of fresh food like chicken, beef, pork chops, fish and veggies. Most meats require no added oil because they're already so juicy: just season them with salt and your favourite herbs and spices. Be sure to use dry seasonings as less moisture gives your food a crispier texture. If you want to baste meats with barbecue sauce or honey, wait until the last couple of minutes of cooking. Lean cuts of meat, or foods with little or no fat, require oil to brown and crisp up. Brush boneless chicken breasts and pork chops with a bit of oil before seasoning. Vegetable oil or canola oil is usually recommended due to its higher smoke point, meaning it can stand up to the high heat in an air fryer.

Vegetables also need to be tossed in oil before air frying. We recommend sprinkling them with salt before air frying, but use a little less than you're used to: The crispy, air fried bits pack a lot of flavour. Try air frying broccoli florets and baby potato halves. Butternut squash and sweet potatoes seem to get sweeter once air fried and green beans and peppers cook very quickly in an Air Fryer.

4 Reasons To Use An Air Fryer

Air frying is increasingly popular because it allows you to quickly and evenly prepare delicious meals with little oil and little effort. Here are just a few of the reasons you'll want to switch to air frying:

- Air Fryers replace other cooking appliances: You can use your Air Fryer instead of several appliances such as your oven, microwave, deep fryer, and dehydrator. In one small device, you can quickly cook up perfect dishes for every meal without sacrificing flavour. You also save energy as you don't have to heat large appliances to cook small meals.
- Air Fryers cook faster than traditional cooking methods: Air frying works by circulating hot air around the cooking basket with fans.

This results in fast and even cooking, using a fraction of the energy of your oven. Most Air Fryers can be set to a maximum temperature of 205°C//400°F Because of this, just about anything you can make in an oven, you can make in an Air Fryer.

- Air Fryers use little to no cooking oil: One of the main selling points of Air Fryers is that you can achieve beautifully cooked foods with little to no cooking oil. While that may be attractive to some because it can mean lower fat content, people following the keto diet can rejoice because it means fewer calories, which still matter if you're doing keto for weight loss. Using an Air Fryer means you can enjoy all the family favourites in a healthy way.
- Air Fryers are fast to clean up: With any method of cooking you're sure to dirty your cooker, but your Air Fryer's smaller cooking chamber and removable basket can be easily cleaned with washing up liquid in the sink or the dishwasher. No more scrubbing stubborn grease stains or oil spills!

Choosing An Air Fryer

When choosing an Air Fryer, the most important things to consider are the size and temperature range. Air fryers are usually measured by litres/quarts which refers to the Air Fryer's capacity and how much food it can hold. A 3-5 litre/quart Air Fryer is suitable for most families. However, a 5-6 litre/quart Air Fryer is perfect for bulk cooking and can fit a whole chicken. If you have a limited amount of kitchen counter or storage space, a smaller sized Air Fryer will be just as useful to have. Use the handy size guide below to help you find the right sized Air Fryer for you and your family.

Air Fryer Size Guide

Size	Capacity
1-2 litre/quart	1-2 people
3-5 litre/quart	2-5 people
6-10 litre/quart	6+ people

If you are interested in also dehydrating your food, look out for Air Fryers that reach low temperatures of around 50°C//120°F for long periods of time. Most Air Fryers are equipped with buttons to allow you to select from several different functions, such as grilling, roasting or baking. These preset functions typically have set times and temperatures set by the Air Fryer manufacturer. Whilst most recipes present manual times and temperatures, some use the low/medium/high-temperature functions so be sure to familiarise yourself with the instructions provided with your Air Fryer by the manufacturer. In most cases, preheating is not necessary unless stated otherwise in the recipe.

You may want to also consider which accessories are included with your Air Fryer as they can enhance the cooking of your food and give you further meal options. Be sure to use tongs and oven mitts when removing the Air Fryer basket or any other accessories. Here are some common Air Fryer accessories:

- Metal holder: This circular rack is used to add a second layer to your cooking surface so you can maximize space and cook multiple things at once. This can be helpful when you're cooking meat and veggies as you can remove the food at different times.
- Skewer rack: Built-in metal skewers that make roasting kebabs super easy.
- Ramekin: Small ramekins are used for making mini cakes and quiches. If they're oven safe, you can safely use them in your Air Fryer.

- Cake pan: Purpose built cake pans fit perfectly into your Air Fryer cooking chamber and have handles you can use to easily pull the pan out when finished baking.
- Cupcake pan: A cupcake pan usually comes with seven mini cups and typically fills a 5 litre/quart Air Fryer. These cups are perfect for muffins and cupcakes. Alternatively, you can also use individual silicone baking cups.
- Parchment: Use pre-cut parchment to make cleanup even easier when baking with your Air Fryer. You can also find parchment paper with precut holes for easy steaming.
- Pizza pan: You can bake a pizza in your Air Fryer using the recipes in this book This is a great option for easily getting the perfect shape every time.

Health Benefits of Using An Air Fryer

As the Air Fryer can produce results similar to deep-frying using a tiny fraction of the oil needed to deep-fry, the health benefits it offers to folks are many. When deep-frying, the food is coated with oil and it is this oil that is absorbed by the food to form a delicious coating on the outside. In an Air Fryer, oil is still used because it helps crisp and brown several foods, but only one tablespoon is generally required at a time. Instead of putting the tablespoon of oil in the Air Fryer, the foods are simply tossed in the fryer with oil and then placed in the Air Fryer basket. In fact, spraying the foods lightly with oil is an even easier way to ensure that foods have an even coating using the least amount of oil. Oil sprays, as opposed to drip oil, are a great way of ensuring this.

Deep-fried foods are considered one of the unhealthiest types of food as they contain relatively higher amounts of fat compared to meals prepared with other cooking methods. By simply using an Air Fryer instead of a deep fat fryer you can reduce the fat content of your favourite meals by up to 75%. This is thanks to the little to no oil used by air fryers instead of the large volumes of oil used by deep fryers. Deep fried meals can use up to 750ml/3 cups of cooking oil, whereas you only need to add about 1 teaspoon of oil to an Air Fryer. Using an air fryer can significantly cut down on the overall fat content of the meals you prepare for your family. You can achieve a similar fried texture and colour of fried food without all the fat by switching to an Air Fryer. Reducing the fat content of your meals will reduce the risk of chronic health conditions, keeping your family fitter for longer.

How To Clean Your Air Fryer

1. Let the Air Fryer cool down properly before cleaning, then unplug the power cord of the Air Fryer.

2. Check the Air Fryer is properly cooled down before cleaning.

3. Clean the outer surface by using a damp towel.

4. Clean the inside of the Air Fryer with a nonabrasive sponge.

5. Clean the basket, crisper plate, and any other accessories in the dishwasher or sink with warm soapy water. Do not clean the main unit in the dishwasher.

6. Any food residue stuck to the basket can be cleaned by placing it in the sink and filling it with soapy warm water for 5 minutes, then removing the residual with a soft sponge.

EXCLUSIVE BONUS

40 Weight Loss Recipes

&

14 Days Meal Plan

Scan the QR-Code and receive
the FREE download:

Breakfast

Fluffy Cheesy Omelette

TIME: 25 MINS | SERVES 2
NET CARBS: 8G | FAT: 14G
PROTEIN: 16G | KCAL: 216

Ingredients

- 4 eggs
- ¼ teaspoon soy sauce
- Freshly ground black pepper, to taste
- 1 large onion, sliced
- 30g//⅛ cup cheddar cheese, grated
- 30g//⅛ cup mozzarella cheese, grated
- Cooking spray

Instructions

1. Preheat the Air Fryer to 180°C//360°F and grease a pan with cooking spray.
2. Whisk together the eggs, soy sauce and black pepper in a bowl.
3. Place onions in the pan and cook for about 10 minutes.
4. Pour the egg mixture over onion slices and top evenly with cheese.
5. Cook for about 5 more minutes and serve.

Tofu Omelette

TIME: 40 MINS | SERVES 2
NET CARBS: 7G | FAT: 16G
PROTEIN: 20G | KCAL: 248

Ingredients

- 2 teaspoons olive oil
- ¼ of onion, chopped
- 1 garlic clove, minced
- 340g//12oz tofu, pressed and sliced
- 1 tablespoon chives, chopped
- 3 eggs, beaten
- Salt and black pepper, to taste

Instructions

1. Preheat the Air Fryer to 180°C//355°F and grease an Air Fryer pan with olive oil.

2. Add onion and garlic to the greased pan and cook for about 4 minutes.

3. Add tofu and chives and season with salt and black pepper.

4. Beat the eggs and pour over the tofu mixture.

5. Cook for about 25 minutes, poking the eggs twice in between.

6. Dish out and serve warm.

Chicken Omelette

TIME: 30 MINS | SERVES 8
NET CARBS: 6G | FAT: 3G
PROTEIN: 14G | KCAL: 161

Ingredients

- 1 teaspoon butter
- 1 onion, chopped
- ½ jalapeño pepper, seeded and chopped
- 35g//¼ cup chicken, cooked and shredded
- 3 eggs
- Salt and black pepper, to taste

Instructions

1. Preheat the Air Fryer to 180°C//355°F and grease an Air Fryer pan.
2. Heat butter in a frying pan over medium heat and add onions.
3. Sauté for about 5 minutes and add jalapeño pepper.
4. Sauté for about 1 minute and stir in the chicken.
5. Remove from the heat and keep aside.
6. Meanwhile, whisk together the eggs, salt, and black pepper in a bowl.
7. Place the chicken mixture into the prepared pan and top with the egg mixture.
8. Cook for about 10 minutes until completely done and serve hot.

Crust-Less Quiche

TIME: 35 MINS | SERVES 2
NET CARBS: 8G | FAT: 24G
PROTEIN: 26G | KCAL: 348

Ingredients

- 4 eggs
- 15g//¼ cup onion, chopped
- 100g//½ cup tomatoes, chopped
- 285ml//½ cup milk
- 240g//1 cup cheddar cheese, shredded
- Salt, to taste

Instructions

1. Preheat the Air Fryer to 170°C//340°F and grease 2 ramekins lightly.
2. Mix all the ingredients together in a ramekin until well combined.
3. Place in the Air Fryer and cook for about 30 minutes.
4. Dish out and serve.

Scrambled Egg

TIME: 20 MINS | SERVES 2
NET CARBS: 25G | FAT: 22G
PROTEIN: 26G | KCAL: 351

Ingredients

- 1 tablespoon butter
- 215ml//¾ cup milk
- 4 eggs
- 8 tomatoes, halved
- 120g//½ cup Parmesan cheese, grated
- Salt and black pepper, to taste

Instructions

1. Preheat the Air Fryer to 180°C//360°F and grease an Air Fryer pan with butter.

2. Whisk together eggs with milk, salt and black pepper in a bowl.

3. Transfer the egg mixture into the prepared pan and place it into the Air Fryer.

4. Cook for about 6 minutes and stir in the tomatoes and cheese.

5. Cook for about 3 minutes and serve warm.

Egg Muffins

TIME: 25 MINS | SERVES 4
NET CARBS: 9G | FAT: 6G
PROTEIN: 3G | KCAL: 251

Ingredients

- 1 egg
- 60g//3.5oz white flour
- 2 tablespoons olive oil
- 1 tablespoon baking powder
- 3 tablespoons milk
- A splash of Worcestershire sauce
- 60g//2oz parmesan, grated

Instructions

1. In a bowl, mix egg with flour, oil, baking powder, milk, Worcestershire and parmesan, whisk well and divide into 4 silicone muffin cups.

2. Arrange cups in your Air Fryer's cooking basket, cover and cook at 200°C//392°F for 15 minutes.

3. Serve warm for breakfast.

Toasties and Sausage in Egg

TIME: 35 MINS | SERVES 2
NET CARBS: 4G | FAT: 19G
PROTEIN: 18G | KCAL: 261

Ingredients

- 3 eggs
- 60g//¼ cup cream
- 1 bread slice, cut into sticks
- 2 cooked sausages, sliced
- 30g//⅛ cup mozzarella cheese, grated
- 30g//⅛ cup Parmesan cheese, grated

Instructions

1. Preheat the Air Fryer to 185°C//365°F and grease 2 ramekins lightly.
2. Whisk together eggs with cream in a bowl and place in the ramekins.
3. Stir in the bread and sausage slices in the egg mixture and top with cheese.
4. Transfer the ramekins to the Air Fryer basket and cook for about 22 minutes.
5. Dish out and serve warm.

Peanut Butter Banana Bread

TIME: 55 MINS | SERVES 6
NET CARBS: 40G | FAT: 3G
PROTEIN: 9G | KCAL: 384

Ingredients

- 125g//1 cup plus 1 tablespoon all-purpose flour
- 1¼ teaspoons baking powder
- ¼ teaspoon salt
- 1 large egg
- 65g//⅓ cup granulated sugar
- 70ml//¼ cup canola oil
- 2 tablespoons sour cream
- 2 tablespoons creamy peanut butter
- 1 teaspoon vanilla extract
- 2 medium ripe bananas, peeled and mashed
- 90g//¾ cup walnuts, roughly chopped

Instructions

1. Preheat the Air Fryer to 165°C//330°F and grease a non-stick baking dish.
2. Mix together the flour, baking powder and salt in a bowl.
3. Whisk together the egg with sugar, canola oil, sour cream, peanut butter and vanilla extract in a bowl.
4. Stir in the bananas and beat until well combined.
5. Now, add the flour mixture and fold in the walnuts gently.
6. Mix until combined and transfer the mixture evenly into the prepared baking dish.
7. Arrange the baking dish in an Air Fryer basket and cook for about 40 minutes.
8. Remove from the Air Fryer and place onto a wire rack to cool.
9. Cut the bread into desired size slices and serve.

Savoury French Toasts

TIME: 15 MINS | SERVES 2
NET CARBS: 27G | FAT: 2G
PROTEIN: 7G | KCAL: 151

Ingredients

- 30g//¼ cup chickpea flour
- 3 tablespoons onion, chopped finely
- 2 teaspoons green chilli, seeded and chopped finely
- Water, as required
- ½ teaspoon red chilli powder
- ¼ teaspoon ground turmeric
- ¼ teaspoon ground cumin
- Salt, to taste
- 4 bread slices

Instructions

1. Preheat the Air Fryer to 190°C//375°F and line an Air Fryer pan with a foil paper.
2. Mix all the ingredients together in a large bowl except the bread slices.
3. Spread the mixture over both sides of the bread slices and transfer into the Air Fryer pan.
4. Cook for about 4 minutes and remove from the Air Fryer to serve.

Potato Hash

TIME: 50 MINS | SERVES 4
NET CARBS: 31G | FAT: 8G
PROTEIN: 10G | KCAL: 229

Ingredients

- 2 teaspoons butter, melted
- 1 medium onion, chopped
- ½ of green bell pepper, seeded and chopped
- 230g//1½oz white potatoes, peeled and cubed
- ½ teaspoon dried thyme, crushed
- ½ teaspoon dried savoury, crushed
- Salt and black pepper, to taste
- 5 eggs, beaten

Instructions

1. Preheat the Air Fryer to 180°C//200°F and grease an Air Fryer pan with melted butter.
2. Put onion and bell pepper in the Air Fryer pan and cook for about 5 minutes.
3. Add the potatoes, thyme, savoury, salt and black pepper and cook for about 30 minutes.
4. Meanwhile, heat a greased skillet on medium heat and stir in the beaten eggs.
5. Cook for about 1 minute on each side and remove from the skillet.
6. Cut it into small pieces and transfer the egg pieces into the Air Fryer pan.
7. Cook for about 5 more minutes and serve warm.

Meat

Mexican Chicken Breast

TIME: 30 MINS | SERVES 2
NET CARBS: 32G | FAT: 18G
PROTEIN: 18G | KCAL: 340

Ingredients

- 230ml//8oz salsa verde
- 230g//½oz boneless, skinless chicken breast
- Salt and black pepper, to taste
- ½ teaspoon garlic powder
- ½ tablespoon olive oil
- 85g//¾ cup cheddar cheese, grated

Instructions

1. Pour salsa verde into a baking dish.
2. Season chicken with salt, pepper, and garlic powder, and brush with olive oil.
3. Place chicken over the salsa verde.
4. Place the baking dish in the Air Fryer and cook at 195°C//380°F for 20 minutes.
5. Sprinkle cheese over the top and cook for 2 more minutes.
6. Serve.

Bacon Wrapped Chicken Breasts

TIME: 45 MINS | SERVES 4
NET CARBS: 3G | FAT: 25G
PROTEIN: 30G | KCAL: 365

Ingredients

- 1 tablespoon palm sugar
- 6-7 Fresh basil leaves
- 2 tablespoons fish sauce
- 2 tablespoons water
- 2 230g//8oz chicken breasts, cut each breast in half horizontally
- Salt and ground black pepper, as required
- 12 bacon strips
- 1½ teaspoon honey

Instructions

1. In a small heavy-bottomed pan, add palm sugar over medium-low heat and cook for about 2-3 minutes or until caramelized, stirring continuously.
2. Add the basil, fish sauce and water and stir to combine.
3. Remove from heat and transfer the sugar mixture into a large bowl.
4. Sprinkle each chicken breast with salt and black pepper.
5. Add the chicken pieces into the sugar mixture and coat generously.
6. Refrigerate to marinate for about 4-6 hours.
7. Set the temperature of the Air Fryer to 185°C//365°F. Grease an Air Fryer Basket.
8. Wrap each chicken piece with 3 bacon strips.
9. Coat each piece slightly with honey.
10. Arrange chicken pieces into the prepared Air Fryer basket.
11. Air Fry for about 20 minutes, flipping once halfway through.
12. Remove from the Air Fryer and transfer the chicken pieces onto a serving platter.
13. Serve hot.

Lime Lamb Mix

TIME: 35 MINS | SERVES 4
NET CARBS: 5G | FAT: 13G
PROTEIN: 15G | KCAL: 284

Ingredients

- 900g//2lb lamb chops
- Juice of 1 lime
- Zest of 1 lime, grated
- A pinch of salt and black pepper
- 1 tablespoon olive oil
- 1 teaspoon sweet paprika
- 1 teaspoon cumin, ground
- 1 tablespoon cumin, ground

Instructions

1. In the Air Fryer's basket, mix the lamb chops with the lime juice and the other ingredients, rub and cook at 195°C//380°F for 15 minutes on each side.
2. Serve with a side salad.

Lamb and Spinach Mix

TIME: 45 MINS | SERVES 6
NET CARBS: 17G | FAT: 6G
PROTEIN: 20G | KCAL: 160

Ingredients

- 450g//1lb lamb meat, cubed
- 450g//1lb spinach
- 400ml//14oz canned tomatoes, chopped
- 2 tablespoons ginger, grated
- 1 red onion, chopped
- 2 teaspoons cardamom, ground
- 2 garlic cloves, minced
- 2 teaspoons cumin powder
- 1 teaspoon garam masala
- ½ teaspoon chilli powder
- 1 teaspoon turmeric
- 2 teaspoons coriander, ground

Instructions

1. In a heatproof dish that fits your Air Fryer, mix lamb with spinach, tomatoes, ginger, garlic, onion, cardamom, cloves, cumin, garam masala, chilli, turmeric and coriander, stir, introduce in preheated Air Fryer and cook at 180°C//360°F for 35 minutes.
2. Divide into bowls and serve.

Smoked Beef Mix

TIME: 25 MINS | SERVES 4
NET CARBS: 6G | FAT: 12G
PROTEIN: 17G | KCAL: 274

Ingredients

- 450g//1lb beef stew meat, roughly cubed
- 1 tablespoon smoked paprika
- 140ml//½ cup beef stock
- ½ teaspoon garam masala
- 2 tablespoons olive oil
- A pinch of salt and black pepper

Instructions

1. In the Air Fryer's basket, mix the beef with the smoked paprika and the other ingredients, toss and cook at 195°C//380°F for 20 minutes on each side.
2. Divide between plates and serve.

Beef Patties and Mushroom Sauce

TIME: 35 MINS | SERVES 6
NET CARBS: 6G | FAT: 23G
PROTEIN: 32G | KCAL: 435

Ingredients

- 900g//2lb beef, ground
- Salt and black pepper to the taste
- ½ teaspoon garlic powder
- 1 tablespoon soy sauce
- 70ml//¼ cup beef stock
- 100g//¾ cup flour
- 1 tablespoon parsley, chopped
- 1 tablespoon onion flakes

For the sauce:

- 50g//1 cup yellow onion, chopped
- 500g//2 cups mushrooms, sliced
- 2 tablespoons bacon fat
- 2 tablespoons butter
- ½ teaspoon soy sauce
- 60g//¼ cup sour cream
- 140ml//½ cup beef stock
- Salt and black pepper to the taste

Instructions

1. In a bowl, mix beef with salt, pepper, garlic powder, soy sauce, beef stock, flour, parsley and onion flakes, stir well, shape into 6 patties, place them in your Air Fryer and cook at 175°C//350°F for 14 minutes.

2. Meanwhile, heat up a pan with the butter and the bacon fat over medium heat, add mushrooms, stir and cook for 4 minutes.

3. Add onions, stir and cook for 4 minutes more.

4. Add ½ teaspoon soy sauce, sour cream and ½ cup stock, stir well, bring to a simmer and take off the heat.

5. Divide beef patties onto plates and serve with mushroom sauce on top.

Greek Beef Mix

TIME: 35 MINS | SERVES 4
NET CARBS: 6G | FAT: 13G
PROTEIN: 15G | KCAL: 283

Ingredients

- 900g//2lb beef stew meat, roughly cubed
- 1 teaspoon coriander, ground
- 1 teaspoon garam masala
- 1 teaspoon cumin, ground
- A pinch of salt and black pepper
- 250g//1 cup Greek yoghurt
- ½ teaspoon turmeric powder

Instructions

1. In the Air Fryer's pan, mix the beef with the coriander and the other ingredients, toss and cook at 195°C//380°F for 30 minutes.
2. Divide between plates and serve.

Chicken Wings

TIME: 35 MINS | SERVES 2
NET CARBS: 0G | FAT: 5G
PROTEIN: 7G | KCAL: 81

Ingredients

- 10 chicken wings (about 700g//1½lb)
- Oil in spray
- 1 tablespoon soy sauce
- ½ tablespoon cornstarch
- 2 tablespoon honey
- 1 tablespoon ground fresh chilli paste
- 1 tablespoon minced garlic
- ½ tablespoon chopped fresh ginger
- 1 tablespoon lime sumo
- ½ tablespoon salt
- 2 tablespoon chives

Instructions

1. Dry the chicken with a tea towel. Cover the chicken with the oil spray.

2. Place the chicken inside the hot air electric fryer, separating the wings towards the edge so that it is not on top of each other. Cook at 195°C//380°F until the skin is crispy for about 25 min. Turn them around half the time.

3. Mix the soy sauce with cornstarch in a small pan. Add honey, chilli paste, garlic, ginger, and lime sumo. Simmer until it boils and thickens. Place the chicken in a bowl, add the sauce and cover all the chicken. Sprinkle with chives.

Pork Chops with Olives and Corn

TIME: 35 MINS | SERVES 4
NET CARBS: 17G | FAT: 8G
PROTEIN: 19G | KCAL: 281

Ingredients

- 900g//2lb pork chops
- 180g//1 cup green olives, pitted and halved
- 180g//1 cup black olives, pitted and halved
- 120g//1 cup corn
- Salt and black pepper to the taste
- 1 tablespoon avocado oil
- 2 tablespoons garlic powder
- 2 tablespoons oregano, dried

Instructions

In the Air Fryer's pan, mix the pork chops with the olives and the other ingredients, toss, cook at 205°C//400°F for 25 minutes, divide between plates and serve.

Beef Casserole

TIME: 1 HR 5 MINS | SERVES 12
NET CARBS: 16G | FAT: 12G
PROTEIN: 15G | KCAL: 200

Ingredients

- 180g//2 cups aubergine//eggplant, chopped
- Salt and black pepper to the taste
- 1 tablespoon olive oil
- 900g//2lb beef, ground
- 2 teaspoons mustard
- 2 teaspoons gluten-free Worcestershire sauce
- 30g//28oz canned tomatoes, chopped
- 450g//2 cups mozzarella, grated
- 450g//16oz tomato sauce
- 2 tablespoons parsley, chopped
- 1 teaspoon oregano, dried

Instructions

1. In a bowl, mix aubergine//eggplant with salt, pepper and oil and toss to coat.

2. In another bowl, mix beef with salt, pepper, mustard and Worcestershire sauce, stir well and spread on the bottom of a pan that fits your Air Fryer.

3. Add aubergine//eggplant mix, tomatoes, tomato sauce, parsley, oregano and sprinkle mozzarella at the end.

4. Introduce in your Air Fryer and cook at 180°C//360°F for 35 minutes.

5. Divide among plates and serve hot.

Fish & Seafood

Sammy Pommel

Crab Cakes

TIME: 50 MINS | SERVES 2
NET CARBS: 5.5G | FAT: 6.5G
PROTEIN: 7G | KCAL: 110

Ingredients

- 1 large egg, beaten
- 1 tablespoon of mayonnaise
- 1 tablespoon Dijon mustard
- 1 tablespoon Worcestershire sauce
- 1 tablespoon all-purpose seasoning
- 1 teaspoon of salt
- A pinch of white pepper
- A pinch of cayenne
- 30g//¼ cup celery, finely diced
- 40g//¼ cup red pepper, finely diced
- 10g//⅛ cup fresh parsley, finely chopped
- 230g//½ lb of crab meat
- 30g//¼ cup breadcrumbs
- Non-Stick Spray Oil

Remodelled:

- 2 teaspoons of mayonnaise
- 20g//⅛ cup capers, washed and drained
- 1 tablespoon sweet pickles, chopped
- 1 tablespoon red onion, finely chopped
- 1 teaspoon of lemon juice
- 1 tablespoon Dijon mustard
- Salt and pepper to taste

Instructions

1. Mix the ingredients of remodelled until everything is well incorporated. Set aside.
2. Beat the egg, mayonnaise, mustard, Worcestershire sauce, all-purpose seasoning, salt, white pepper, cayenne pepper, celery, pepper, and parsley.
3. Gently stir the crab meat in the egg mixture and stir it until well mixed.
4. Sprinkle the breadcrumbs over the crab mixture and fold them gently until the breadcrumbs cover every corner.
5. Shape the crab mixture into 4 cakes and chill in the fridge for 30 minutes.
6. Select Preheat in the Air Fryer and press Start/Pause.
7. Place a sheet of baking paper in the basket of the preheated Air Fryer.
8. Sprinkle the crab cakes with cooking spray and place them gently on the paper.
9. Cook the crab cakes at 205°C//400°F for 8 minutes until golden brown.
10. Flip crab cakes during cooking.
11. Serve with remodelled.

Tuna Pie

TIME: 40 MINS | SERVES 4
NET CARBS: 21G | FAT: 14G
PROTEIN: 9G | KCAL: 244

Ingredients

- 2 hard-boiled eggs
- 2 tuna cans
- 200ml//7oz fried tomato
- 1 sheet of broken dough.

Instructions

1. Cut the eggs into small pieces and mix with the tuna and tomato.

2. Spread the sheet of broken dough and cut into two equal squares.

3. Put the mixture of tuna, eggs, and tomato on one of the squares.

4. Cover with the other, join at the ends and decorate with leftover little pieces.

5. Preheat the Air Fryer for a few minutes at 180°C//350°F.

6. Enter in the Air Fryer basket and set the timer for 15 minutes at 180°C//350°F.

Tuna-Stuffed Jacket Potatoes

TIME: 25 MINS | SERVES 4
NET CARBS: 15G | FAT: 13G
PROTEIN: 26G | KCAL: 281

Ingredients

- 4 starchy potatoes, soaked for about 30 minutes and drain
- 1 (170g//6oz) can tuna, drained
- 2 tablespoons plain Greek yoghurt
- 1 scallion, chopped and divided
- 1 tablespoon capers
- ½ tablespoon olive oil
- 1 teaspoon red chilli powder
- Salt and black pepper, to taste

Instructions

1. Preheat the Air Fryer to 180°C//350°F and grease an Air Fryer basket.
2. Arrange the potatoes in the Air Fryer basket and cook for about 30 minutes.
3. Meanwhile, mix tuna, yoghurt, red chilli powder, salt, black pepper and half of the scallion in a bowl and mash the mixture well.
4. Remove the potatoes from the Air Fryer and halve the potatoes lengthwise carefully.
5. Stuff in the tuna mixture in the potatoes and top with capers and remaining scallion.
6. Dish out on a platter and serve immediately.

Tuna Puff Pastry

TIME: 20 MINS | SERVES 2
NET CARBS: 26G | FAT: 16G
PROTEIN: 8G | KCAL: 291

Ingredients

- 2 square puff pastry dough, bought ready
- 1 egg (white and yolk separated)
- 140ml//½ cup tuna tea
- 140ml//½ cup chopped parsley tea
- 100g//½ cup chopped tea olives
- Salt and pepper to taste

Instructions

1. Preheat the Air Fryer. Set the timer to 5 minutes and the temperature to 200°C//390°F.

2. Mix the tuna with olives and parsley. Season to taste and set aside. Place half of the filling in each dough and fold in half. Brush with egg white and close gently. After closing, make two small cuts at the top of the air outlet.

3. Brush with the egg yolk.

4. Place in the basket of the Air Fryer. Set the time to 10 minutes and press the power button.

Fish Tacos

TIME: 17 MINS | SERVES 4-5
NET CARBS: 11G | FAT: 26G
PROTEIN: 9G | KCAL: 108

Ingredients

- 450g//1lb of tilapia, cut into strips of 38mm//1.5inch thick
- 60g//⅓ cup yellow cornmeal
- 1 teaspoon ground cumin
- 1 teaspoon chilli powder
- 1 teaspoon garlic powder
- 1 teaspoon onion powder
- 1 teaspoon of salt
- 1 teaspoon black pepper
- Non-Stick Spray Oil
- Corn tortillas, to serve
- Tartar sauce, to serve
- Lime wedges, to serve

Instructions

1. Cut the tilapia into strips 38 mm//1.5inch thick.
2. Mix cornmeal and seasonings in a shallow dish.
3. Cover the fish strips with seasoned cornmeal. Set aside in the fridge.
4. Preheat the Air Fryer for 5 minutes. Set the temperature to 170°C//340°F.
5. Sprinkle the fish coated with oil spray and place it in the preheated Air Fryer.
6. Put the fish in the Air Fryer, and set the timer to 7 minutes.
7. Turn the fish halfway through cooking.
8. Serve the fish in corn tortillas with tartar sauce and a splash of lemon.

Salmon and Veggie Patties

TIME: 35 MINS | SERVES 6
NET CARBS: 45G | FAT: 12G
PROTEIN: 12G | KCAL: 334

Ingredients

- 1 (170g//6oz) salmon fillet
- 3 large russet potatoes, boiled and mashed
- 1 egg
- 75g//1 cup frozen vegetables, parboiled and drained
- 2 tablespoons dried parsley, chopped
- 1 teaspoon dried dill, chopped
- Salt and freshly ground pepper, to taste
- 120g//1 cup breadcrumbs
- 70ml//¼ cup olive oil

Instructions

1. Preheat the Air Fryer to 170°C//335°F and line a pan with foil paper.
2. Place salmon in the Air Fryer basket and cook for about 5 minutes.
3. Dish out the salmon in a large bowl and flake with a fork.
4. Mix potatoes, egg, parboiled vegetables, parsley, dill, salt and black pepper until well combined.
5. Make 6 equal sized patties from the mixture and coat the patties evenly with breadcrumbs.
6. Drizzle with the olive oil and arrange the patties in the pan.
7. Transfer into the Air Fryer basket and cook for about 12 minutes, flipping once in between.

Salmon Fillets

TIME: 15 MINS | SERVES 7
NET CARBS: 0.1G | FAT: 4G
PROTEIN: 13G | KCAL: 88

Ingredients

- 2 (200g//7oz) (90mm//¾-inch thick) salmon fillets
- 1 tablespoon Italian seasoning
- 1 tablespoon fresh lemon juice

Instructions

1. Preheat the Air Fryer to 180°C//355°F and grease an Air Fryer grill pan.

2. Rub the salmon evenly with Italian seasoning and transfer into the Air Fryer grill pan, skin-side up.

3. Cook for about 7 minutes and squeeze lemon juice on it to serve.

Steamed Salmon with Dill Sauce

TIME: 25 MINS | SERVES 2
NET CARBS: 4G | FAT: 14G
PROTEIN: 21G | KCAL: 224

Ingredients

- 285ml//1 cup water
- 2 (170g//6oz) salmon fillets
- 140g//½ cup Greek yoghurt
- 2 tablespoons fresh dill, chopped and divided
- 2 teaspoons olive oil
- Salt, to taste
- 140g//½ cup sour cream

Instructions

1. Preheat the Air Fryer to 140°C//285°F and grease an Air Fryer basket.
2. Place water into the bottom of the Air Fryer pan.
3. Coat salmon with olive oil and season with a pinch of salt.
4. Arrange the salmon in the Air Fryer and cook for about 11 minutes.
5. Meanwhile, mix the remaining ingredients in a bowl to make dill sauce.
6. Serve the salmon with dill sauce.

Cod Cakes

TIME: 30 MINS | SERVES 4
NET CARBS: 16G | FAT: 3G
PROTEIN: 19G | KCAL: 171

Ingredients

- 450g//1lb cod fillets
- 1 teaspoon fresh lime zest, grated finely
- 1 egg
- 1 teaspoon red chilli paste
- Salt, to taste
- 1 tablespoon fresh lime juice
- 30g//1/3 cup coconut, grated and divided
- 1 scallion, chopped finely
- 2 tablespoons fresh parsley, chopped

Instructions

1. Preheat the Air Fryer to 190°C//375°F and grease an Air Fryer basket.
2. Put cod filets, lime zest, egg, chilli paste, salt and lime juice in a food processor and pulse until smooth.
3. Transfer the cod mixture to a bowl and add 2 tablespoons coconut, scallion and parsley.
4. Make 12 equal sized round cakes from the mixture.
5. Put the remaining coconut in a shallow dish and coat the cod cakes in it.
6. Arrange 6 cakes in the Air Fryer basket and cook for about 7 minutes.
7. Repeat with the remaining cod cakes and serve warm.

Prawns and Sweet Potato

TIME: 40 MINS | SERVES 4
NET CARBS: 52G | FAT: 4G
PROTEIN: 11G | KCAL: 285

Ingredients

- 1 shallot, chopped
- 1 red chilli pepper, seeded and chopped finely
- 12 king prawns, peeled and deveined
- 5 large sweet potatoes, peeled and cut into slices
- 4 lemongrass stalks
- 2 tablespoons dried rosemary
- 70g//⅓ cup olive oil, divided
- 4 garlic cloves, minced
- Smoked paprika, to taste
- 1 tablespoon honey

Instructions

1. Preheat the Air Fryer to 180°C//355°F and grease an Air Fryer basket.
2. Mix olive oil, shallot, red chilli pepper, garlic and paprika in a bowl.
3. Add prawns and coat evenly with the mixture.
4. Thread the prawns onto lemongrass stalks and refrigerate to marinate for about 3 hours.
5. Mix sweet potatoes, honey and rosemary in a bowl and toss to coat well.
6. Arrange the potatoes in the Air Fryer basket and cook for about 15 minutes.
7. Remove the sweet potatoes from the Air Fryer and set the Air Fryer to 200°C//390°F.
8. Place the prawns in the Air Fryer basket and cook for about 5 minutes.
9. Dish out in a bowl and serve with sweet potatoes.

Quick and Easy Shrimp

TIME: 15 MINS | SERVES 2
NET CARBS: 0.3G | FAT: 8.3G
PROTEIN: 24G | KCAL: 174

Ingredients

- 225g//½lb tiger shrimp
- 1 tablespoon olive oil
- ½ teaspoon all-purpose seasoning
- ¼ teaspoon smoked paprika
- ¼ teaspoon cayenne pepper
- Salt, to taste

Instructions

1. Preheat the Air Fryer to 200°C//390°F and grease an Air Fryer basket.
2. Mix all the ingredients in a large bowl until well combined.
3. Place the shrimps in the Air Fryer basket and cook for about 5 minutes.
4. Dish out and serve warm.

Side Dishes

Beans and Rice

TIME: 1 HR 15 MINS | SERVES 4
NET CARBS: 77G | FAT: 6G
PROTEIN: 20G | KCAL: 440

Ingredients

- 425ml//1½ cups boiling water
- 425g//15oz kidney beans, dark red, undrained
- ½ teaspoon marjoram leaves, dried
- 110g//½ cup cheddar cheese, shredded
- 210g//1 cup white rice, long grain, uncooked
- 1 tablespoon chicken/vegetable stock, granulated
- 1 onion, medium, chopped
- 255g//9oz butter beans, drained

Instructions

1. Preheat Air Fryer at 160°C//325°F.
2. Combine all ingredients, save for cheese, in a casserole.
3. Cover and air-fry for one hour and fifteen minutes. Give the dish a stir before topping with cheese.

Cheesy Potato Mash Casserole

TIME: 1HR 35 MINS | SERVES 24
NET CARBS: 18G | FAT: 2.5G
PROTEIN: 4G | KCAL: 110

Ingredients

- 2.3kg//5lb white potatoes, peeled, cubed
- 55g/ ¼ cup parmesan cheese, shredded
- 220g//1 cup cheddar cheese, reduced fat, shredded
- 85g//3oz cream cheese, reduced fat, softened
- 55g//¼ cup Blue cheese, crumbled
- 1 teaspoon garlic salt
- 245g//1 cup yoghurt, plain, fat-free
- 1 teaspoon chives, fresh, chopped
- 1/4 teaspoon paprika

Instructions

1. Place potatoes in a saucepan filled with water. Heat to boiling, then cook on simmer for fifteen to eighteen minutes.
2. Beat together parmesan cheese, cheddar cheese, cream cheese, and blue cheese until smooth. Beat in garlic salt and yoghurt.
3. Preheat Air Fryer to 160°C//325°F.
4. Mash cooked potatoes until smooth. Stir in the cheese mixture. Add to a baking dish and air-fry for 35-40 minutes.

Squash Casserole

TIME: 60 MINS | SERVES 6
NET CARBS: 12G | FAT: 5G
PROTEIN: 4G | KCAL: 110

Ingredients

- 210g//1 cup brown rice, cooked
- 25g//½ cup onion, diced
- 1 plum tomato, diced
- ½ teaspoon salt
- ⅛ teaspoon pepper
- 1 tablespoon thyme leaves, fresh, chopped
- 1 squash, medium, sliced thinly
- 1 courgette/zucchini, medium, sliced thinly
- 120g//½ cup Italian cheese blend, gluten-free, shredded
- 1 tablespoon olive oil, extra virgin

Instructions

1. Preheat Air Fryer to 190°C//375°F.
2. Mist cooking spray onto a casserole dish.
3. Combine rice, onion, tomato, pepper, salt (¼ teaspoon), oil, and ½ thyme leaves. Spread evenly into a casserole dish and layer on top with squash and courgette//zucchini. Sprinkle with remaining salt (¼ teaspoon) and thyme.
4. Cover and air-fry for 20 minutes. Top with cheese and air-fry for another 10-12 minutes.

Ginger Pork Lasagna

TIME: 1 HR 30 MINS | SERVES 8
NET CARBS: 37G | FAT: 24G
PROTEIN: 28G | KCAL: 480

Ingredients

- 1 tablespoon butter
- 450g//1lb ground pork
- 1 tablespoon sesame oil, toasted
- 4 green onion greens & whites, separated, sliced thinly
- 1 tablespoon ginger root, fresh, minced
- 1 tablespoon fish sauce
- 1 tablespoon chilli garlic sauce
- 425ml//15oz tomato sauce
- 140ml//½ cup coconut milk
- 2 garlic cloves, minced
- 425g//15oz ricotta cheese, part skim
- 48 dumpling pastry wrappers, square
- 1 tablespoon parmesan cheese, shredded
- 2 tablespoons Thai basil leaves, fresh, sliced thinly

Instructions

1. Preheat the Air Fryer to 160°C//325°F degrees Fahrenheit.
2. Mist cooking spray onto a baking dish.
3. In a skillet heated on medium, cook pork in butter and sesame oil for eight to ten minutes. Stir in garlic, green onion whites, and ginger root and cook for one to two minutes. Stir in fish sauce, chilli garlic sauce, and tomato sauce.
4. Cook on a gentle simmer.
5. Combine coconut milk, ricotta cheese, and parmesan cheese.
6. Arrange 8 overlapping dumpling pastry wrappers into a baking dish to line the bottom, then top with a second layer of eight wrappers. Spread on top ⅓ of cheese mixture and layer with ⅓ of pork mixture. Repeat layering twice and finish by topping with parmesan cheese.
7. Cover the dish with foil and air-fry for thirty minutes. Remove foil and air-fry for another ten to fifteen minutes.
8. Serve topped with basil and green onion greens.

Baked Sweet Potatoes

TIME: 20MINS | SERVES 2
NET CARBS: 4G | FAT: 2G
PROTEIN: 4G | KCAL: 152

Ingredients

- 2 big sweet potatoes, scrubbed
- 285ml//1 cup water
- A pinch of salt and black pepper
- ½ teaspoon smoked paprika
- ½ teaspoon cumin, ground

Instructions

1. Put the water in your pressure cooker, add the steamer basket, add sweet potatoes inside, cover and cook on High for 10 minutes.
2. Split potatoes, add salt, pepper, paprika and cumin, divide them between plates and serve as a side dish.

Broccoli Pasta

TIME: 15 MINS | SERVES 2
NET CARBS: 77G | FAT: 6G
PROTEIN: 20G | KCAL: 440

Ingredients

- 570ml//2 cups water
- 225g//½lb pasta
- 225g//8oz cheddar cheese, grated
- 35g//½ cup broccoli
- 140ml//½ cup half and half

Instructions

1. Put the water and the pasta in your pressure cooker.
2. Add the steamer basket, add the broccoli, cover the cooker and cook on High for 4 minutes.
3. Drain the pasta, transfer it, as well as the broccoli, and clean the pot.
4. Set it on sauté mode, add pasta and broccoli, cheese and half and half, stir well, cook for 2 minutes, divide between plates and serve as a side dish for chicken.

Cauliflower Rice

TIME: 20 MINS | SERVES 2
NET CARBS: 4G | FAT: 1G
PROTEIN: 5G | KCAL: 191

Ingredients

- 1 tablespoon olive oil
- ½ cauliflower head, florets separated
- A pinch of salt and black pepper
- A pinch of parsley flakes
- ¼ teaspoon cumin, ground
- ¼ teaspoon turmeric powder
- ¼ teaspoon paprika
- 285ml//1 cup water
- ½ tablespoon cilantro, chopped
- Juice from ⅓ lime

Instructions

1. Put the water in your pressure cooker, add the steamer basket, add cauliflower florets, cover and cook on High for 2 minutes.
2. Discard water, transfer cauliflower to a plate and leave aside.
3. Clean your pressure cooker, add the oil, set on sauté mode and heat it up.
4. Add cauliflower, mash using a potato masher, add salt, pepper, parsley, cumin, turmeric, paprika, cilantro and lime juice, stir well, cook for 10 minutes more, divide between 2 plates and serve as a side dish.

Roasted Potatoes

TIME: 35 MINS | SERVES 2
NET CARBS: 8G | FAT: 1G
PROTEIN: 8G | KCAL: 192

Ingredients

- 225g//½lb potatoes, cut into wedges
- ¼ teaspoon onion powder
- ½ teaspoon garlic powder
- 2 tablespoons avocado oil
- A pinch of salt and black pepper
- 140ml//½ cup chicken stock

Instructions

1. Set your pressure cooker on sauté mode, add the oil and heat it up.
2. Add potatoes, onion powder, garlic powder, salt and pepper, stir and sauté for 8 minutes.
3. Add stock, cover and cook on High for 7 minutes more.
4. Divide between 2 plates and serve as a side dish.

Squash Risotto

TIME: 25 MINS | SERVES 2
NET CARBS: 3G | FAT: 1G
PROTEIN: 6G | KCAL: 163

Ingredients

- 1 small yellow onion, chopped
- A drizzle of olive oil
- 1 garlic clove, minced
- ½ red bell pepper, chopped
- 200g//1 cup butternut squash, chopped
- 210g//1 cup risotto rice
- 425ml//1½ cups veggie stock
- 3 tablespoons dry white wine
- 120g//4oz mushrooms, chopped
- A pinch of salt and black pepper
- A pinch of oregano, dried
- ¼ teaspoon coriander, ground
- 35g//1½ cups mixed kale and spinach
- 1 tablespoon nutritional yeast

Instructions

1. Set your pressure cooker on sauté mode, add the oil and heat it up.
2. Add onion, bell pepper, squash and garlic, stir and cook for 5 minutes.
3. Add rice, stock, wine, salt, pepper, mushrooms, oregano and coriander, stir, cover and cook on High for 5 minutes.
4. Add mixed kale and spinach, parsley and yeast, stir and leave aside for 5 minutes.
5. Divide between 2 plates and serve as a side dish.

Spanish Rice

TIME: 20 MINS | SERVES 2
NET CARBS: 6G | FAT: 1G
PROTEIN: 8G | KCAL: 174

Ingredients

- ½ tablespoon olive oil
- ½ tablespoon butter
- 100g//½ cup rice
- 140ml//½ cup chicken stock
- 140ml//½ cup tomato sauce
- 1 teaspoon chilli powder
- ½ teaspoon cumin, ground
- ¼ teaspoon oregano, dried
- A pinch of salt and black pepper
- 2 tablespoons tomatoes, chopped

Instructions

1. Put the oil in your pressure cooker, set on sauté mode and heat it up.
2. Add rice, stir and cook for 4 minutes.
3. Add stock, tomato sauce, chilli powder, cumin, oregano, tomatoes, salt and pepper, stir, cover and cook on High for 8 minutes.
4. Stir rice one more time, divide between 2 plates and serve as a side dish.

Carrots and Kale

TIME: 20 MINS | SERVES 2
NET CARBS: 6G | FAT: 2G
PROTEIN: 8G | KCAL: 183

Ingredients

- 280g//10oz kale, roughly chopped
- 1 tablespoon butter
- 3 carrots, sliced
- 1 yellow onion, chopped
- 4 garlic cloves, minced
- 140ml//½ cup chicken stock
- A pinch of salt and black pepper
- A splash of balsamic vinegar
- ¼ teaspoon red pepper flakes

Instructions

1. Set your pressure cooker on sauté mode, add butter and melt it.
2. Add onion and carrots, stir and cook for 3 minutes.
3. Add garlic, stir and cook for 1 minute more.
4. Add kale and stock, cover and cook on High for 7 minutes.
5. Add vinegar and pepper flakes, stir, divide between 2 plates and serve.

Snacks

Spicy Chicken Breasts

TIME: 30 MINS | SERVES 2
NET CARBS: 15G | FAT: 6G
PROTEIN: 15G | KCAL: 135

Ingredients

- 2 large eggs, whisked
- 2 tablespoons lemon juice
- Salt and black pepper
- 450g//1lb of chicken breast
- 120g//1 cup breadcrumbs
- 1 teaspoon smoked paprika
- ¼ teaspoon garlic powder
- ¼ teaspoon onion powder
- 120g//½ cup fresh grated parmesan cheese

Instructions

1. Preheat the unit by selecting AIR FRY mode for 2 minutes at 160°C//325°F.
2. Select START/PAUSE to begin the preheating process.
3. Once preheating is done, press START/PAUSE.
4. Take a bowl and whisk eggs in it and set it aside for further use.
5. In a large bowl add lemon juice, paprika, salt, black pepper, garlic powder, onion powder.
6. In a separate bowl mix breadcrumbs and parmesan cheese.
7. Dip the chicken breasts in the spice mixture and coat the entire breast well.
8. Let the tenders sit for 1 hour.
9. Then dip each chicken breast in egg and then in bread crumbs.
10. Line the basket of the Air Fryer with parchment paper.
11. Transfer the tenders to the basket.
12. Set it to air fry mode at 175°C//350°F for 12 minutes.
13. Serve with ketchup.

Parmesan Chicken

TIME: 40 MINS | SERVES 4
NET CARBS: 11G | FAT: 5G
PROTEIN: 25G | KCAL: 174

Ingredients

- 4 chicken breasts
- 235g//1 cup parmesan cheese
- 120g//1 cup breadcrumbs
- 2 eggs, whisked
- Salt, to taste
- Oil spray, for greasing

Instructions

1. Preheat the unit by selecting AIR FRY mode for 5 minutes at 160°C//325°F.
2. Select START/PAUSE to begin the preheating process.
3. Once preheating is done, press START/PAUSE.
4. Whisk egg in a large bowl and set aside.
5. Season the chicken breast with salt and then put it in egg wash.
6. Next, dredge it in breadcrumbs and parmesan cheese.
7. Line the basket of the Air Fryer with parchment paper.
8. Put the breast pieces inside the basket, and oil spray the breast pieces.
9. Set it to air fry mode at 175°C//350°F, for 18 minutes.
10. Serve with ketchup.

Stuffed Bell Peppers

TIME: 40 MINS | SERVES 3
NET CARBS: 18G | FAT: 6G
PROTEIN: 25G | KCAL: 105

Ingredients

- 6 large bell peppers
- 300g//1½ cup cooked rice
- 470g//2 cups cheddar cheese

Instructions

1. Preheat the unit by selecting AIR FRY mode for 5 minutes at 175°C//350°F.
2. Select START/PAUSE to begin the preheating process.
3. Once preheating is done, press START/PAUSE.
4. Cut the bell peppers in half lengthwise and remove all the seeds.
5. Fill the cavity of each bell pepper with cooked rice.
6. Grease the basket of Air Fryer with oil spray.
7. Transfer the bell peppers to the basket of the Ninja Air Fryer.
8. Set the time for 90°C//200°F for 10 minutes.
9. Afterwards, take out the basket and sprinkle cheese on top.
10. Set the time at 90°C//200°F for 6 minutes.
11. Once it's done, serve.

Air Fry Cheese Sandwich

TIME: 25 MINS | SERVES 2
NET CARBS: 15G | FAT: 8G
PROTEIN: 18G | KCAL: 157

Ingredients

- 4 slices of white bread slices
- 2 tablespoons of butter, melted
- 2 slices of sharp cheddar
- 2 slices of Swiss cheese
- 2 slices of mozzarella cheese

Instructions

1. Preheat the unit by selecting AIR FRY mode for 2 minutes at 160°C//325°F.
2. Select START/PAUSE to begin the preheating process.
3. Once preheating is done, press START/PAUSE.
4. Brush melted butter on one side of all the bread slices and then top the 2 bread slices with slices of cheddar, Swiss, and mozzarella, one slice per bread.
5. Top it with the other slice to make a sandwich.
6. Add it to the basket of the Air Fryer.
7. Turn on AIR FRY mode at 175°C//350°F for 10 minutes.
8. Once done, serve.

Cheddar Quiche

TIME: 25 MINS | SERVES 2
NET CARBS: 6G | FAT: 2G
PROTEIN: 8G | KCAL: 183

Ingredients

- 4 eggs, organic
- 360g//1½ cup heavy cream
- Salt, pinch
- 35g//½ cup broccoli florets
- 120g//½ cup cheddar cheese, shredded and for sprinkling

Instructions

1. Take a Pyrex pitcher and crack two eggs in it.
2. And fill it with heavy cream, about half the way up.
3. Add in the salt and then add in the broccoli and pour this into a quiche dish, and top it with shredded cheddar cheese.
4. Preheat the unit by selecting AIR FRY mode for 2 minutes at 160°C//325°F.
5. Select START/PAUSE to begin the preheating process.
6. Once preheating is done, press START/PAUSE.
7. Now put the dish inside the Air Fryer basket.
8. Set the time to 12 minutes at 160°C//325°F.
9. Once done, serve hot.

Sweet Bites

TIME: 35 MINS | SERVES 4
NET CARBS: 15G | FAT: 7G
PROTEIN: 11G | KCAL: 197

Ingredients

- 10 sheets of Phyllo dough, (filo dough)
- 2 tablespoons of melted butter
- 125g//1 cup walnuts, chopped
- 2 teaspoons of honey
- Pinch of cinnamon
- 1 teaspoon of orange zest

Instructions

1. Preheat the unit by selecting AIR FRY mode for 2 minutes at 160°C//325°F.
2. Select START/PAUSE to begin the preheating process.
3. Once preheating is done, press START/PAUSE.
4. First, layer together 10 Phyllo dough sheets on a flat surface. Then cut it into 4 1cm//4inch squares.
5. Now, coat the squares with butter, drizzle some honey, orange zest, walnuts, and cinnamon.
6. Bring all 4 corners together and press the corners to make a little purse design.
7. Put it inside the Air Fryer basket and select the AIR fry mode and set it for 10 minutes at 190°C//375°F.
8. Once done, take out and with a topping of nuts.

Pizza Rolls

TIME: 35 MINS | SERVES 8
NET CARBS: 2.5G | FAT: 24G
PROTEIN: 21G | KCAL: 233

Ingredients

- 450//2 cups shredded mozzarella cheese
- 60g//½ cup almond flour
- 2 large eggs
- 72 slices pepperoni
- 8 (30g//1oz) mozzarella string cheese sticks, cut into 3 pieces each
- 2 tablespoons unsalted butter, melted
- ¼ teaspoon garlic powder
- ½ teaspoon dried parsley
- 2 tablespoons grated Parmesan cheese

Instructions

1. In a large microwave-safe bowl, place mozzarella and almond flour. Microwave for 1 minute. Remove bowl and mix until a ball of dough forms. Microwave additional 30 seconds if necessary.

2. Crack eggs into the bowl and mix until a smooth dough ball forms. Wet your hands with water and knead the dough briefly.

3. Tear off two large pieces of parchment paper and spray one side of each with nonstick cooking spray. Place the dough ball between the two sheets, with sprayed sides facing the dough. Use a rolling pin to roll the dough out to //¼ inch thickness.

4. Use a knife to slice into 24 rectangles. On each rectangle place 3 pepperoni slices and 1 piece of string cheese.

5. Fold the rectangle in half, covering pepperoni and cheese filling. Pinch or roll sides closed. Cut a piece of parchment to fit your Air Fryer basket and place it into the basket. Put the rolls onto the parchment.

6. Adjust the temperature to 175°C//350°F and set the timer for 10 minutes.

7. After 5 minutes, open the fryer and flip the pizza rolls. Restart the fryer and continue cooking until pizza rolls are golden.

8. In a small bowl, place butter, garlic powder, and parsley. Brush the mixture over cooked pizza rolls and then sprinkle with Parmesan. Serve warm.

Mozzarella Sticks

TIME: 1 HR 10 MINS | SERVES 4
NET CARBS: 5G | FAT: 13G
PROTEIN: 19G | KCAL: 136

Ingredients

- 6 (30g//1oz) mozzarella string cheese sticks
- 120g//½ cup grated Parmesan cheese
- 15g//½ oz pork rinds, finely ground
- 1 teaspoon dried parsley
- 2 large eggs

Instructions

1. Place mozzarella sticks on a cutting board and cut them in half. Freeze for 45 minutes or until firm. If freezing overnight, remove frozen sticks after 1 hour and place them into an airtight zip-top storage bag and place them back in the freezer for future use.
2. In a large bowl, mix Parmesan, ground pork rinds, and parsley.
3. In a medium bowl, whisk eggs.
4. Dip a frozen mozzarella stick into beaten eggs and then into the Parmesan mixture to coat. Repeat with remaining sticks. Place mozzarella sticks into the Air Fryer basket.
5. Adjust the temperature to 205°C//400°F and set the timer for 10 minutes or until golden.
6. Serve warm.

Crustless Three-Meat Pizza

TIME: 10 MINS | SERVES 2
NET CARBS: 4G | FAT: 24G
PROTEIN: 18G | KCAL: 266

Ingredients

- 120g//½ cup shredded mozzarella cheese
- 7 slices pepperoni
- 35g//¼ cup cooked ground sausage
- 2 slices sugar-free bacon, cooked and crumbled
- 1 tablespoon grated Parmesan cheese
- 2 tablespoons low-carb, sugar-free pizza sauce, for dipping

Instructions

1. Cover the bottom of a 15cm//6inch cake pan with mozzarella. Place pepperoni, sausage, and bacon on top of the cheese and sprinkle with Parmesan. Place the pan into the Air Fryer basket.

2. Adjust the temperature to 205°C//400°F and set the timer for 5 minutes.

3. Remove when the cheese is bubbling and golden. Serve warm with pizza sauce for dipping.

Beef Jerky

TIME: 4 HRS 5 MINS | SERVES 10
NET CARBS: 1G | FAT: 3G
PROTEIN: 10G | KCAL: 85

Ingredients

- 450g//1lb flat iron beef, thinly sliced
- 70ml//¼ cup soy sauce (or liquid aminos)
- 2 teaspoons Worcestershire sauce
- ¼ teaspoon crushed red pepper flakes
- ¼ teaspoon garlic powder
- ¼ teaspoon onion powder

Instructions

1. Place all ingredients into a plastic storage bag or covered container and marinate for 2 hours in the refrigerator.
2. Place each slice of jerky on the Air Fryer rack in a single layer.
3. Adjust the temperature to 70°C//160°F and set the timer for 4 hours.
4. Cool and store in an airtight container for up to 1 week.

Dessert

Buttermilk Biscuits

TIME: 25 MINS | SERVES 4
NET CARBS: 45G | FAT: 18G
PROTEIN: 7G | KCAL: 374

Ingredients

- 65g//½ cup cake flour
- 155g//1¼ cups all-purpose flour
- ¾ teaspoon baking powder
- 70ml//¼ cup + 2 tablespoons butter, cut into cubes
- 215ml//¾ cup buttermilk
- 1 teaspoon granulated sugar
- Salt, to taste

Instructions

1. Preheat the Air fryer to 205°C//400°F and grease a pie pan lightly.
2. Sift together flours, baking soda, baking powder, sugar and salt in a large bowl.
3. Add cold butter and mix until a coarse crumb is formed.
4. Stir in the buttermilk slowly and mix until a dough is formed.
5. Press the dough into 13mm//½inch thickness onto a floured surface and cut out circles with a 45mm//1¾inch round cookie cutter.
6. Arrange the biscuits in a pie pan in a single layer and brush butter on them.
7. Transfer into the Air fryer and cook for about 8 minutes until golden brown.

Blueberry Bowls

TIME: 25 MINS | SERVES 4
NET CARBS: 14G | FAT: 2G
PROTEIN: 7G | KCAL: 230

Ingredients

- 380g//2 cups blueberries
- 285ml//1 cup coconut water
- 2 tablespoons sugar
- 2 teaspoons vanilla extract
- Juice of ½ lime

Instructions

In your Air Fryer's pan, combine the blueberries with the water and the other ingredients, toss and cook at 160°C//320°F for 12 minutes.

Carrot Brownies

TIME: 35 MINS | SERVES 8
NET CARBS: 12G | FAT: 12G
PROTEIN: 5G | KCAL: 230

Ingredients

- 1 teaspoon almond extract
- 2 eggs, whisked
- 140g//½ cup butter, melted
- 4 tablespoons sugar
- 250g//2 cups almond flour
- 50g//½ cup carrot, peeled and grated

Instructions

1. In a bowl, combine the eggs with the butter and the other ingredients, whisk, spread this into a pan that fits your Air Fryer, introduce into the fryer and cook at 170°C//340°F for 25 minutes.
2. Cool down, slice and serve.

Carrot Bread

TIME: 50 MINS | SERVES 6
NET CARBS: 13G | FAT: 5G
PROTEIN: 7G | KCAL: 200

Ingredients

- 220g//2 cups carrots, peeled and grated
- 200g//1 cup sugar
- 3 eggs, whisked
- 250g//2 cups white flour
- 1 tablespoon baking soda
- 285ml//1 cup almond milk

Instructions

1. In a bowl, combine the carrots with the sugar and the other ingredients, whisk well, pour this into a lined loaf pan, introduce the pan in the Air Fryer and cook at 170°C//340°F for 40 minutes.
2. Cool the bread down, slice and serve.

Yoghurt Cake

TIME: 40 MINS | SERVES 8
NET CARBS: 11G | FAT: 13G
PROTEIN: 5G | KCAL: 231

Ingredients

- 6 eggs, whisked
- 1 teaspoon vanilla extract
- 1 teaspoon baking soda
- 255g//9oz almond flour
- 4 tablespoons sugar
- 500g//2 cups yoghurt

Instructions

1. In a blender, combine the eggs with the vanilla and the other ingredients, pulse, spread into a cake pan lined with parchment paper, put it in the Air Fryer and cook at 165°C//330°F for 30 minutes.
2. Cool the cake down, slice and serve.

Pear Pudding

TIME: 30 MINS | SERVES 6
NET CARBS: 14G | FAT: 4G
PROTEIN: 6G | KCAL: 211

Ingredients

- 3 tablespoons sugar
- 140ml//½ cup butter, melted
- 2 eggs, whisked
- 2 pears, peeled and chopped
- 95//⅓ cup almond milk
- 120g//½ cup heavy cream

Instructions

1. In a bowl, combine the butter with the sugar and the other ingredients, whisk well and pour into a pudding pan.
2. Introduce the pan to the Air Fryer and cook at 170°C//340°F for 20 minutes.
3. Cool the pudding down, divide into bowls and serve.

Lime Cake

TIME: 40 MINS | SERVES 4
NET CARBS: 15G | FAT: 5G
PROTEIN: 6G | KCAL: 213

Ingredients

- 1 egg, whisked
- 2 tablespoons sugar
- 2 tablespoons butter, melted
- 140ml//½ cup almond milk
- 2 tablespoons lime juice
- 1 tablespoon lime zest, grated
- 240g//1 cup heavy cream
- ½ teaspoon baking powder

Instructions

1. In a bowl, combine the egg with the sugar, butter and the other ingredients, whisk well and transfer to a cake pan lined with parchment paper.
2. Put the pan in your Air Fryer and cook at 160°C//320°F for 30 minutes.
3. Serve the cake cold.

Avocado Cake

TIME: 20 MINS | SERVES 4
NET CARBS: 8G | FAT: 1G
PROTEIN: 2G | KCAL: 171

Ingredients

- 2 avocados, peeled, pitted and mashed
- 480g//2 cups heavy cream
- 2 tablespoons sugar
- 1 tablespoon lemon juice

Instructions

1. In a blender, combine the avocados with the cream and the other ingredients, pulse well, divide into 4 ramekins, introduce them into the fryer and cook at 160°C//320°F for 10 minutes.

2. Serve the cream really cold.

Cake with Strawberries & Cream

TIME: 25 MINS | SERVES 2
NET CARBS: 32G | FAT: 8G
PROTEIN: 2G | KCAL: 213

Ingredients

- 1 pure butter puff pastry to stretch
- 500g//18oz strawberries (clean and without skin)
- 1 bowl of custard
- 3 tbsp icing sugar baked at 210°C//410°F in the Air Fryer

Instructions

1. Unroll the puff pastry and place it on the baking sheet. Prick the bottom with a fork and spread the custard. Arrange the strawberries in a circle and sprinkle them with icing sugar.
2. Cook in a fryer setting a 120°C//250°F for 15 minutes.
3. Remove the cake from the fryer with the tongs and let cool.
4. When serving, sprinkle icing sugar with whipped cream.

Apple Pie

TIME: 1 HR 30 MINS | SERVES 3
NET CARBS: 57G | FAT: 20G
PROTEIN: 4G | KCAL: 311

Ingredients

- 600g//5 cups flour
- 350g//1 ½ cups margarine
- 150g//¾ cup sugar
- 2 eggs
- 50g// ⅓ cup breadcrumbs
- 3 apples
- 75g// ½ cup raisins
- 1 teaspoon Cinnamon

Instructions

1. Put the flour, sugar, eggs, and margarine nuts in the blender just outside the refrigerator.

2. Mix everything until you get a compact and quite flexible mixture. Let it rest in the refrigerator for at least 30 minutes.

3. Preheat the Air Fryer at 150°C//305°F for 5 minutes.

4. Spread ⅔ of the mass of broken dough in 3mm//0.1inch thick covering the previously floured and floured tank and making the edges adhere well, which should be at least 2 cm.

5. Place the breadcrumbs, apple slices, sugar, raisins, and cinnamon in the bottom; cover everything with the remaining dough and make holes in the top to allow steam to escape.

6. Cook for 40 minutes and then turn off the lower resistance.

7. Cook for another 20 minutes only with the upper resistance on. Once it has cooled, put it on a plate and serve.

Vegetarian

Spinach Cheese Pie

TIME: 30 MINS | SERVES 4
NET CARBS: 4G | FAT: 20G
PROTEIN: 18G | KCAL: 288

Ingredients

- 225g//1 cup frozen chopped spinach, drained
- 60g//¼ cup heavy whipping cream
- 240g//1 cup shredded sharp Cheddar cheese
- 15g//¼ cup diced yellow onion
- 6 large eggs

Instructions

1. Take a medium bowl, whisk eggs and add cream. Add the remaining ingredients to the bowl.

2. Pour into a 15cm//6-inch round baking dish. Place into the Air Fryer basket. Adjust the temperature to 160°C//320°F and set the timer for 20 minutes.

3. Eggs will be firm and slightly browned when cooked. Serve immediately.

Garlic Tomatoes

TIME: 20 MINS | SERVES 4
NET CARBS: 4G | FAT: 3G
PROTEIN: 6G | KCAL: 121

Ingredients

- 450g//1lb cherry tomatoes; halved
- 6 garlic cloves; minced
- 1 tablespoon olive oil
- 1 tablespoon dill; chopped
- 1 tablespoon balsamic vinegar
- Salt and black pepper to taste

Instructions

1. In a pan that fits the Air Fryer, combine all the ingredients, and toss gently.
2. Put the pan in the Air Fryer and cook at 190°C//380°F for 15 minutes.
3. Divide between plates and serve.

Broccoli and Almonds

TIME: 20 MINS | SERVES 4
NET CARBS: 4G | FAT: 4G
PROTEIN: 6G | KCAL: 180

Ingredients

- 450g//1lb broccoli florets
- 55g//½ cup almonds, chopped
- 3 garlic cloves, minced
- 1 tablespoon chives, chopped
- 2 tablespoons red vinegar
- 3 tablespoons coconut oil, melted
- A pinch of salt and black pepper

Instructions

1. Take a bowl and mix the broccoli with the garlic, salt, pepper, vinegar and the oil and toss.

2. Put the broccoli in your Air Fryer's basket and cook at 190°C//380°F for 12 minutes.

3. Divide between plates and serve with almonds and chives sprinkled on top.

Turmeric Cabbage

TIME: 20 MINS | SERVES 4
NET CARBS: 6G | FAT: 5G
PROTEIN: 7G | KCAL: 173

Ingredients

- 1 green cabbage head, shredded
- 70ml//¼ cup ghee; melted
- 1 tablespoon. dill; chopped
- 2 tablespoon turmeric powder

Instructions

1. In a pan that fits your Air Fryer, mix the cabbage with the rest of the ingredients except the dill, toss, put the pan in the fryer and cook at 190°C//370°F for 15 minutes.

2. Divide everything between plates and serve with dill sprinkled on top.

Parmesan Artichokes

TIME: 20 MINS | SERVES 4
NET CARBS: 10G | FAT: 14G
PROTEIN: 8G | KCAL: 189

Ingredients

- 30g//¼ cup blanched finely ground almond flour
- 2 medium artichokes, trimmed and quartered, centre removed
- 1 large egg, beaten
- 120g//½ cup grated vegetarian Parmesan cheese
- 2 tablespoon coconut oil
- ½ teaspoon crushed red pepper flakes

Instructions

1. Take a large bowl, toss artichokes in coconut oil and then dip each piece into the egg.
2. Mix the Parmesan and almond flour in a large bowl. Add artichoke pieces and toss to cover as completely as possible, sprinkle with pepper flakes.
3. Place into the Air Fryer basket.
4. Adjust the temperature to 205°C//400°F and set the timer for 10 minutes.
5. Toss the basket two times during cooking. Serve warm.

Roasted Broccoli Salad

TIME: 15 MINS | SERVES 2
NET CARBS: 12G | FAT: 16G
PROTEIN: 6G | KCAL: 215

Ingredients

- 210g//3 cups fresh broccoli florets
- ½ medium lemon
- 25g//¼ cup sliced almonds
- 2 tablespoon salted butter; melted

Instructions

1. Place broccoli into a 15cm//6inch round baking dish. Pour butter over the broccoli.
2. Add almonds and toss. Place dish into the Air Fryer basket.
3. Adjust the temperature to 195°C//380°F and set the timer for 7 minutes.
4. Stir halfway through the cooking time. When the timer beeps, zest lemon onto broccoli and squeeze the juice into the pan. Toss. Serve warm.

Kale and Bell Peppers

TIME: 15 MINS | SERVES 4
NET CARBS: 4G | FAT: 3G
PROTEIN: 5G | KCAL: 131

Ingredients

- 300g//1½ cups avocado, peeled, pitted and cubed
- 45g//2 cups kale, torn
- 70ml//¼ cup olive oil
- 150g//1 cup red bell pepper; sliced
- 1 tablespoon white vinegar
- 2 tablespoon lime juice
- 1 tablespoon mustard
- A pinch of salt and black pepper

Instructions

1. In a pan that fits the Air Fryer, combine the kale with salt, pepper, avocado and half of the oil, and toss.
2. Put in your Air Fryer and cook at 180°C//360°F for 10 minutes.
3. In a bowl, combine the kale mix with the rest of the ingredients, toss and serve.

Mini Mushroom Pizzas

TIME: 20 MINS | SERVES 2
NET CARBS: 7G | FAT: 19G
PROTEIN: 10G | KCAL: 244

Ingredients

- 2 large portobello mushrooms
- 2 leaves of fresh basil; chopped
- 150g//⅔ cup shredded mozzarella cheese
- 4 grape tomatoes, sliced
- 1 tablespoon balsamic vinegar
- 2 tablespoon unsalted butter; melted
- ½ teaspoon garlic powder

Instructions

1. Scoop out the inside of the mushrooms, leaving just the caps. Brush each cap with butter and sprinkle with garlic powder.

2. Fill each cap with mozzarella and sliced tomatoes. Place each mini pizza into a 5cm//6inch round baking pan. Place the pan into the Air Fryer basket.

3. Adjust the temperature to 190°C//380°F and set the timer for 10 minutes.

4. Carefully remove the pizzas from the fryer basket and garnish with basil and a drizzle of vinegar.

Frying Potatoes

TIME: 45 MINS | SERVES 4
NET CARBS: 48G | FAT: 17G
PROTEIN: 4G | KCAL: 265

Ingredients

- 5 to 6 medium potatoes
- Olive oil in a spray bottle if possible
- Mill salt
- Freshly ground pepper

Instructions

1. Wash the potatoes well and dry them.
2. Brush with a little oil on both sides if not with the oil.
3. Crush some ground salt and pepper on top.
4. Place the potatoes in the fryer basket.
5. Set the cooking at 190°C//380°F for 40 minutes, in the middle of cooking turn the potatoes for even cooking on both sides.
6. At the end of cooking, remove the potatoes from the basket, cut them in half and slightly scrape the melting potato inside and add only a little butter, and enjoy!

Avocado Fries

TIME: 15 MINS | SERVES 2
NET CARBS: 24G | FAT: 32G
PROTEIN: 4G | KCAL: 390

Ingredients

- 1 egg
- 1 ripe avocado
- ½ tsp salt
- 60g//½ cup of panko breadcrumbs

Instructions

1. Preheat the Air Fryer to 200°C//400°F for 5 minutes.
2. Remove the avocado pit and cut it into fries. In a small bowl, whisk the egg with the salt.
3. Enter the breadcrumbs on a plate.
4. Dip the quarters in the egg mixture, then in the breadcrumbs.
5. Put them in the fryer. Cook for 8-10 minutes.
6. Turn halfway through cooking.

Crispy French Fries

TIME: 15 MINS | SERVES 2
NET CARBS: 36G | FAT: 9G
PROTEIN: 3G | KCAL: 240

Ingredients

- 2 medium sweet potatoes
- 2 tsp olive oil
- ½ teaspoon salt
- ½ teaspoon garlic powder
- ¼ teaspoon paprika
- Black pepper

Instructions

1. Preheat the hot Air Fryer to 200°C//400°F.
2. Spray the basket with a little oil.
3. Cut the sweet potatoes into potato chips about 1 cm wide.
4. Add oil, salt, garlic powder, pepper and paprika.
5. Cook for 8 minutes, without overloading the basket.
6. Repeat 2 or 3 times, as necessary.

Frying Potatoes with Butter

TIME: 15 MINS | SERVES 2
NET CARBS: 48G | FAT: 17G
PROTEIN: 4G | KCAL: 365

Ingredients

- 2 Russet potatoes
- Butter
- Fresh parsley (optional)

Instructions

1. Spray the basket with a little oil.
2. Open your potatoes along.
3. Make some holes with a fork.
4. Add the butter and parsley.
5. Transfer to the basket. If your Air Fryer to a temperature of 198°C//390°F.
6. Cook for 30 to 40 minutes.
7. Serve whilst hot.

EXCLUSIVE BONUS

40 Weight Loss Recipes

&

14 Days Meal Plan

Scan the QR-Code and receive
the FREE download:

Disclaimer

This book contains opinions and ideas of the author and is meant to teach the reader informative and helpful knowledge while due care should be taken by the user in the application of the information provided. The instructions and strategies are possibly not right for every reader and there is no guarantee that they work for everyone. Using this book and implementing the information/recipes therein contained is explicitly your own responsibility and risk. This work with all its contents, does not guarantee correctness, completion, quality or correctness of the provided information. Misinformation or misprints cannot be completely eliminated.

Printed in Great Britain
by Amazon

86026595R00064